The Real Scientist

Flash!

Light and how we see things

Peter Riley

W
FRANKLIN WATTS
LONDON • SYDNEY

Contents

Light energy 4

5 How to be a real scientist

Lights out! 6

Clever cameras 8

Bouncing rays 10

Magical mirrors 12

See above your head 14

Leabharlanna Dhún Laoghaire · Ráth An Dúin

Kaleidoscope crazy  16

 Bending light 18

Magnify me!  20

 Rainbow light 22

Colour crazy 24

Results and answers 28

Further information 30

Glossary 31

Index 32

Light for sight 26

Light energy

What do we see when lightning strikes or fireworks explode in the sky? **FLASH!** There's a burst of light! Everything we see is as a result of light streaming into our eyes. No one is sure exactly what light is, because it behaves in different ways. But real scientists know that light is a form of energy. Most of the light energy that lights up our world comes from the Sun.

Light shoots across the air in an instant, moving at 300,000 metres per second straight into our eyes! Light energy is released by the Sun and other stars. It is also released when materials, like these fireworks, burn or glow.

Sometimes light energy travels in waves. When sea waves crash together they get mixed up. The rainbow colours we see on a bubble surface happen when light waves collide.

At other times light behaves like microscopic cannon balls called photons. When photons crash into light cells, such as the ones in this solar-powered mobile phone charger, they generate electricity.

How to be a real scientist

Real scientists look at our world and try to understand it by thinking about it and performing experiments. You can be a real scientist too! Just look at each topic, read the 'getting going' section and then get experimenting.

Set up a science box
Find a large box, then skip through the pages in this book and look at the things you need for getting going and for each activity. Collect them up and put them in your science box.

Use these science skills

▶ **Observe**
Look carefully at whatever you are investigating.

▶ **Predict**
Guess what will happen before you experiment.

▶ **A fair test**
If you are comparing how light behaves, make sure you keep everything the same in your tests except for one thing, such as the way you shine the light.

▶ **Science notebook**
You will need a science notebook in which to put information about your investigations.

▶ **Record**
Write down what happened and perhaps make a drawing in your science notebook. You could take photographs too or make a video using a camcorder or mobile phone.

▶ **Make a conclusion**
Compare what happened with your prediction and see if you were right. It does not matter if you were wrong because it helps you rethink your ideas.

▶ **Experiments and answers**
Follow the steps in the experiments carefully. Use your science skills. There may be extra experiments and a question for you to try. Check all your observations, ideas and answers on pages 28–29.

▶ **What went wrong?**
Science experiments are famous for going wrong – sometimes. If your experiment does not seem to work, look for this section to help you make it right.

Lights out!

Light isn't everywhere all the time. At night, the Sun leaves the sky and it becomes dark. Even in the daytime there are dark shadows. Look around you on a sunny day and you'll see your shadow. Shadows are places where some light cannot reach. They form on the side of objects that is away from the light source.

▼ These laser beams are as straight as a ruler, just like all light rays.

▼ You can often guess what something is from its shadow!

Light travels in straight lines, called rays. When light rays meet an opaque object, they cannot pass through or go round it, so a dark shadow is left on the other side. Translucent and transparent objects form weak or no shadows because they let some – or all – light through.

Getting going

Shadows shift as the Sun moves around the sky. Stand on a pavement at different times of day and get a friend to draw round your shadow in chalk. How does it change? Now try experimenting with some more shadow shapes.

1 Place the block at the edge of a sheet of paper. Shine the torch at it, from about 20 cm away. Move the torch closer, then further away.

Science box

Small torch, wooden block (e.g. domino), sheets of white paper, glue, cereal box, protractor, ruler and pen, felt-tips or coloured pencils, collection of small objects (e.g. toy figure, toy car, marble), clear plastic cup or bottle.

2 On a clean piece of paper, use the protractor and ruler to draw lines at angles of 30, 40, 50, 60, 70, 80 and 90 degrees. Stick the paper on the side of a cereal packet.

▶ **Observe**
Draw around the shadows in each step, using different colours. How do the shadows change each time? Can you create some cool shadow patterns on the paper? Try taking photographs of the shadows and see if your friends can guess the objects' identity.

▶ **Predict**
What would happen if you replaced the block with a clear plastic cup or bottle? Test your prediction.

▶ **Record**
Make a table and record the length of the shadow when the torch is shone at the block from 30, 40, 50, 60, 70, 80 and 90 degrees.

3 Line up the cereal packet with the block. Shine the torch on the block at each angle in turn, starting at 30 degrees.

▶ **Fair test**
Keep the torch at the same distance from the object as you change the angle at which it shines.

▶ **Extra experiment**
Shine a large torch at a white wall or screen in a darkened room. Make shapes with your hands in front of the light. Can you make a bird or a deer shadow? Try other animals!

4 Place an object in the centre of a piece of paper and shine the torch at it from one height but different directions. Try using other objects.

▶ **Think about it**
What would happen if you shone two torches on an object from different directions?

Clever cameras

Cameras are amazing light machines! They take in light and use it to make a picture, or photograph. When light energy enters a digital camera, it creates currents of electricity. These form a picture that is stored in the camera's memory when you click the button.

▼ Most mobile phones have a digital camera. You can use one to record your experimenting!

Getting going

The simplest camera is a pinhole camera. It lets in just a few rays of light through a tiny hole. The rays travel in a straight line to a screen at the back, where they form a faint but clear picture. Can you make a picture using a pinhole camera?

1

Paint the inside of the box black and leave it to dry. Cut a large window in one end of the box, leaving a narrow frame around the edge.

2

Cut a smaller window in the other end, about 6 cm square. Put on the lid and seal it down with sticky tape so that no light can get in.

Science box

Shoe box (or other similar-sized card box) with a lid, black poster paint, paintbrush, sticky tape, scissors, greaseproof paper, aluminium foil, drawing pin, torch.

3

Tape a piece of greaseproof paper over the large window and a piece of foil over the small window.

4

Use a drawing pin to make a tiny hole in the centre of the foil. Be very careful not to tear the foil.

▶ Observe
Switch on the torch and point the foil end of the camera at the light. What do you see on the grease-proof paper. Move the camera closer. Describe what you see. Point the foil end of the camera at a sunny window (but not the Sun).

▶ What's wrong?
Can't see the sunny window? Put a shade around the screen. Make sure the box is properly sealed. Still can't see anything? Make the pinhole slightly larger.

▶ Predict
What would happen if you made the hole bigger? What would happen if you made two holes? Test your predictions.

▶ Think about it
Our eyes act like pinhole cameras to make pictures of the world. Which way up are these pictures at the back of our eyes?

Bouncing rays

Things that give out light are called light sources. They include candles, light bulbs, stars and computer screens, as well as the big one – the Sun! But most things in our world don't produce light – so how do we see them? We see them by light rays bouncing off them. Real scientists call this reflection.

You are reading this by light rays reflecting off the page into your eyes. The light source might be an electric light, or it might be sunlight through a window. Light from the Sun will have bounced off many things, such as clouds, walls and trees, before reaching you.

Getting going

Some materials reflect light better than others. Try bouncing light off your watch onto the ceiling and making it dance around! Could you do the same with your bare arm? Let's find out more about reflecting.

1 Use lumps of modelling clay to stand up the two white cards. Arrange them with the torch between, so that light reflects from one card onto the other.

2 Move the second card slowly away from the other. When you can no longer see the light reflected on it, measure the distance between the cards.

◀ **Rays from the lights at this fairground are bouncing off the rides, and lighting up the surroundings.**

Science box

Torch, modelling clay, 10 cm square of each of the following: 2 pieces of white card, 2 pieces of aluminium foil, sandpaper, coloured paper (including black), shiny wrapping paper, newspaper, glue, tape measure, black polythene.

▶ Observe

Look at the reflected light that falls on the second white card. See how it changes as you move the card. Which material has the most light-bouncing power? Which has the least?

▶ What's wrong?

Light not shining on the second card? Move the first card to make a different angle with the second.

▶ Predict

What would happen if you reflected the light off a piece of black polythene? Test your prediction.

▶ Record

Make a bar chart using your measurements. The biggest bar will belong to the material with the most reflective power. Make up a points system for the most and least reflective materials.

▶ Fair test

Move the card very slowly and stop as soon as the light spot disappears. Keep the torch and sample card in the same place each time.

▶ Think about it

What is the path of the light from the torch to your eye as you look at the way each sample reflects light?

3

Stick aluminium foil to the first card and shine the light on it from the same place. Repeat the moving and measuring you did in step 2. Try again with a wrinkled piece of foil.

4

Stick each of the papers in your collection onto the card in turn and shine the light on them. Move and measure as before.

Magical mirrors

When light rays bounce off an object onto a mirror, something unusual happens. All the rays are reflected back in line. If you look into the mirror you see a picture, or image, of the object. You might think the image is just like the object, but it isn't! In fact it is a wrong-way-round, or reversed, view of the real thing.

▼ The picture that you see in a mirror is the wrong-way-round. Look in this convex mirror – you can see the photographer!

If you move up close to a mirror, your image seems to be just behind the glass. If you move back, it seems further away. Real scientists call these 'virtual images'.

▼ Wobbly mirrors create strange reflections because the light bounces off in all directions.

Getting going

You may have noticed that the writing on the front of some ambulances is back-to-front. This is so that people looking in their car mirrors can read it easily. Try reading this page reflected in a mirror. Tricky? Now try making some mirror writing of your own.

1 Draw a simple shape, such as a star, on a sheet of paper. Stand the mirror behind it (or prop the mirror against a wall).

2 Looking only in the mirror, NOT at the paper, try drawing over the shape with a different coloured pen.

3 Place a clean piece of paper in front of the mirror. Again looking only in the mirror, try writing your name so it looks like normal writing in the mirror.

4 Write the word CHOICE in neat capital letters and place it in front of the mirror. What do you see?

Science box
Sheets of white paper, felt-tips or markers, mirror, large spoon.

▶ **Observe**
Try writing a word in mirror writing without looking in the mirror. Test it in the mirror. What do you see if you look at mirror writing from the back of the paper? Can you work out an easy way to do mirror writing from this?

▶ **Predict**
In step 4, what other words do you think would look the same on the paper and in the mirror? Test your prediction.

▶ **Record**
Make a table listing each letter of the alphabet with its mirror image beside it. Do this for both small and capital letters. You can use the mirror letters to write in code!

▶ **Fair test**
Don't cheat by looking at your hands when you are making mirror writing.

▶ **Extra experiment**
Test what happens to shapes when you look at them in a curved mirror, such as a spoon. Look at the spoon from both sides.

▶ **Think about it**
The curved-out (convex) surface on a spoon spreads out light rays. What happens to the rays when they strike the curved-in (concave) surface?

See above your head

What happens if you reflect the image in one mirror into another mirror? When the light rays reach the second mirror, they form the image again. You can use this idea to look at places above your head! In World War I, soldiers invented a device called a periscope to do just that.

In a periscope, two mirrors are fitted into a tube. You look into the bottom mirror, while the top mirror takes in the view.

▲ Periscopes are useful in crowds. Even if there are lots of people in front of you, you can still see the action by looking over their heads.

▲ Submarines use periscopes to help them see what's going on above the water.

Getting going

You can use two mirrors to see to your side. Hold one mirror in front of you in your left hand and turn it so you can see a mirror held in your right hand. Use the two mirrors to see out of a window while you're facing a wall. Now make a periscope to see above your head.

1

Turn your box on its side and measure the width. Mark this distance from the top of the box down one side. Draw a line from the mark to the opposite top corner of the box.

Science box

Tall juice carton or other long, narrow box, scissors, two small plastic mirrors (as wide as the box), ruler, pen.

2

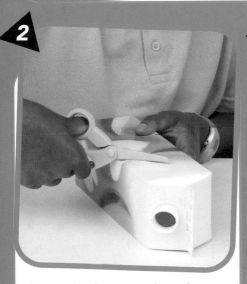

3

Slot in a mirror, facing into the box. Cut a window in the front of the box near the top, so you can see the mirror.

Turn the box over and repeat on the opposite side. Make sure the line goes in the same direction as the first. Cut a slit along each line.

4

Turn the box around and repeat steps 1–3 at the bottom end.

▶ **Observe**
Look at an object with the periscope. Can you see it clearly? Can you use the periscope to see over a wall or someone's head?

▶ **Fair test**
Stay in the same position when you look through both periscopes.

▶ **Think about it**
How could you make a periscope to see behind you?

▶ **Extra experiment**
Join two boxes together to make a periscope twice as long. Look at the same object through both periscopes. Which gives the clearest view?

▶ **What's wrong?**
Can't see a picture with your periscope? Check that the mirrors are correctly lined up.

Kaleidoscope crazy

By bouncing an image between two mirrors you can create some fun effects. If the mirrors are facing each other with an object inbetween, the image of the object is repeated many, many times, getting smaller until it seems to disappear. If the mirrors are at an angle, a limited number of images are produced.

▲ **This image is from a kaleidoscope. By twisting the end of the kaleidoscope tube you can produce lots of different patterns.**

Nearly 200 years ago, a real scientist called Sir David Brewster was experimenting with mirrors in a tube when he discovered they could make beautiful patterns. From his experiments he invented the kaleidoscope. It became a popular toy!

Getting going

Take two small plastic mirrors and hinge them together with sticky tape. Place them at right angles and put a pencil between them. What do you see? You can make a kaleidoscope in a similar way.

▲ **The image of this daisy flower is repeated in these drops of water.**

Cool kaleidoscope

1 Mark out two lines on the back of the mirror card, 7 cm from each long edge.

Science box

1 sheet each of mirror card and holographic mirror card 21 cm x 23 cm (from a craft store), pencil, ruler, scissors, sticky tape, clear plastic freezer bag, coloured paper, sticky tape, confetti, sequins and any other sparkly shapes, torch.

2 Fold along the lines to make a triangular tube with the mirrors on the inside. Join up with sticky tape.

▶ **Observe**
Point the kaleidoscope at a window (but not at the Sun) and look through the centre of the open end. What do you see? Move your eye to each corner of the open end and look again. Twist the kaleidoscope. What do you see?

▶ **Predict**
What would you see if you put coloured paper in the bag instead of sparkly bits or sequins? Test your prediction.

3 Cut off a corner of the freezer bag to give a triangular pocket. Put sparkly shapes inside the plastic triangle.

▶ **Extra experiment**
Repeat the steps using holographic card. Look down through the tube and shine a torch into the lower end from one side, so the light shines onto only one mirror surface. What do you see? What do you see if you move the torch around?

▶ **What's wrong?**
Tube is more like a cylinder than a triangular shape? Bend the card more strongly at the folds.

4 Seal the edge of the pocket with sticky tape and attach it to one end of the mirror tube.

▶ **Think about it**
Hold two mirrors at a 45 degree angle to each other and place a pen in between them. How many reflections do you see? How could you make more reflections?

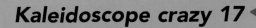

Bending light

We've seen that light whizzes through the air in perfect straight lines. But when it goes through transparent materials, such as water or glass, it slows down a little. When light changes speed, it can also change direction – it's as if the light rays are being bent. Real scientists call this refraction. Look out – it can play tricks with your eyes!

◀ **This brush in water looks broken at the surface. In fact, the light rays have been bent by refraction.**

▼ **If the light hits the surface at a right angle it carries on in a straight line...**

2

1

...but if it strikes at any other angle (1), the ray is refracted. When the light ray comes back out into the air (2), it is refracted again as it speeds up then carries on in a straight line.

Getting going

Refraction in a swimming pool makes the water look shallower than it really is. Light rays coming from the bottom of the pool bend when they move out of the water into the air, so they appear to have come from just below the surface. Let's see how water makes light bend.

Watery wiggle

1

Cut two pieces of cardboard and stick them to the face of the torch with a narrow slit between. When you switch on the torch it should give a thin beam of light.

Science box

Torch, cardboard, sticky tape, clear, square-sided jar or small tub, water, large sheet of black paper, protractor, white pencil, ruler, bowl, coin.

2

Draw a white line across the middle of the black paper. Use a protractor to draw lines at 30, 50, 70 and 90 degrees from the middle of this line.

3

Fill the jar with water and place it on the paper, with the front edge along your first pencil line. Draw a line along the back edge of the jar.

4

Darken the room and point the torch at the jar so the beam shines along the 50 degree pencil line. Look down at the beam coming out of the jar at the other side.

▶ **Observe**
Draw a line along the beam leaving the jar. Measure the angle of this line from the jar edge. Shine the torch along a different angle line and repeat.

▶ **Predict**
What would happen if you shone the torch along the 90 degree line? Test your prediction.

▶ **Record**
Make a table comparing the angle of the beam going in with the angle of the beam coming out. What do you notice?

▶ **Extra experiment**
Put a coin in the bottom of a bowl and position yourself so the coin is just out of your sight. Get a friend to very slowly fill the bowl with water. What do you see?

▶ **Think about it**
Why could it be dangerous to cross a river just by looking at the bottom and not testing the depth with a stick?

Bending light 19

Magnify me!

Real scientists can do clever things with refraction using lenses. A lens is a disc of glass or plastic, with surfaces that curve out or curve in. When light passes through, the rays are refracted. Lenses can be made to focus light to help people see more clearly.

▲ A microscope has lenses in it to make small things like tiny insects seem BIG!

▲ An optician can fit glasses with lenses that are specially made to help people with vision problems.

Getting going

Lenses that curve out are called convex. Lenses that curve in are concave. Telescopes and binoculars use different combinations of lenses to bring distant subjects into focus. Try making your own simple telescope!

1 NEVER LOOK DIRECTLY AT THE SUN. Look through one magnifying glass and hold the other one out in front. Move the magnifying glasses back and forth until you can focus on a distant object through them. Get a friend to measure how far apart the magnifying glasses are.

Science box

2 magnifying glasses (one larger than the other works best), tape measure or ruler, 2 large sheets of card, pencil, scissors, sticky tape.

2 Roll up a piece of card to make a tube the length of your measurement and as wide as the first magnifying glass. Secure it with sticky tape.

3 Cut a slot in the top of the tube, about 2 cm from the end. Push the first magnifying glass into the slot. This is your eyepiece.

4 Make another card tube (the same length) that slides easily over the first tube. Make a slot, as above, for the other magnifying glass to fit into. Slip this tube over the eyepiece tube.

▶**Observe**
Look into the eyepiece lens and shut the other eye. Slide the bigger tube back and forth until an object comes into focus. What do you notice?

▶**What's wrong?**
Whatever you are looking at doesn't appear much closer? Open the eye that's not looking into the telescope and compare what you see.

▶**Extra experiment**
Use a magnifying glass to look at the words on this page. What do you see? What might happen if you look through the second lens at the first one.

▶**Think about it**
What have you made in the extra experiment? Long-sighted people have difficulty focusing on things close-up. Which type of lens focuses light inwards to correct this?

Rainbow light

If you watch the spray from a hosepipe on a sunny day, you may see colours in the water drops. Light rays from the Sun are refracted as they enter the drops – but this time they don't just bend. Inside the drops they bounce around and collide with other refracted rays, splitting into light waves of different colours – the spectrum.

▲ A real scientist called Isaac Newton discovered the spectrum in c.1660. He shone sunlight through a glass prism onto a screen, but you can see it here in these CDs.

◀ Sunlight is actually made up of seven colours – red, orange, yellow, green, blue, indigo and violet. You can see them in a rainbow.

Getting going

Most of the time we see sunlight as white light – all the colours mixed together. You can split light into colours by shining it at the playing side of a CD. Now try doing the opposite – make the colours blend to white!

When light strikes most objects, some of the colours are absorbed by the object and some are reflected. We see the reflected colours. A tomato, for example, takes in most colours but reflects red. Objects that reflect all the colours appear white and objects that absorb all the colours appear black.

Wheel of wonder

1 Draw around the CD on the card and cut out the circle.

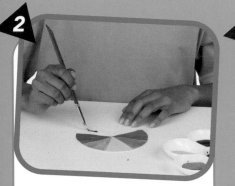

Science box

Stiff white card, pencil, CD or other round template, scissors, protractor, coloured paints (red, orange, yellow, green, blue, indigo, violet), string (about 1 m long).

2 Use a protractor to divide the circle into eight equal segments (each angle should be 45 degrees). Paint seven of the segments, each with a different rainbow colour.

3  Carefully pierce two small holes through the centre of the colour wheel. Thread the string or twine through the holes and knot the ends together.

4 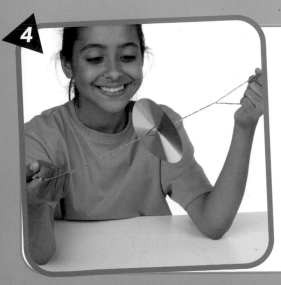 Pull the wheel to the middle of the string. Flip it over and over until the whole string is twisted tightly. Then make a sharp tug on each end of the string and watch the wheel spin!

▶ **Observe**
What do you see when you spin the wheel? Make other wheels using just two or three colours. What do you see when they spin?

▶ **Predict**
What will you see if you use red and green segments only? What if you use blue and yellow? Test your predictions.

▶ **What's wrong?**
Wheel doesn't spin properly? Try sticking it to a thicker piece of cardboard.

▶ **Record**
Make a table of the colour combinations on the wheels and the colours you saw when you spun them.

▶ **Fair test**
Make sure the colour segments are equally sized.

▶ **Extra experiment**
Look at a magazine picture through a strong magnifying glass or microscope. What do you see?

▶ **Think about it**
A television picture is made up of tiny dots of light in just three colours – red, blue and green. How do they make a full-colour scene?

Colour crazy

You can change the way the world looks by stopping some of the colours reaching your eyes. That's what happens when you use a light filter. If you look through something clear but coloured, like a sweet wrapper, you see only the colours it lets through. If the filter blocks blue light, you won't see blue objects through it – they'll look black!

Coloured filters are used on theatre spotlights. When light shines through red filters they bathe the stage in red light and make the scene look warm. If blue and purple filters are used, the scene looks cold.

Getting going

Photographers often use light filters when they are taking pictures outdoors. Try looking at the sky through a red or orange cellophane sweet wrapper. Does it look sunnier? Now be a real scientist and investigate some more.

Coloured glass makes a wonderful light display.

1 Cut the card into pieces about 8 cm x 6 cm. Cut a window in each rectangle, about 6 cm x 4 cm. Stick a piece of different coloured cellophane over each window.

Science box

Card, scissors, pieces of cellophane (coloured red, blue, green and yellow), sticky tape, old CD, piece of white paper, red pencil, selection of coloured items such as an orange, lemon, tomato, green apple, two torches, sticky tape.

2 Turn the CD disc so that it catches the light and makes a spectrum on its surface. Look at the spectrum through each filter in turn.

3 Look at the collection of coloured objects through each filter in turn. Place each object on the white paper in turn.

4 Draw a picture with the red pencil and then look at it with the red filter.

▶ **Observe**
What did you see when you looked at the spectrum with the red filter? What did you see when you used the blue filter? What did you see when you looked at the red picture through the red filter?

▶ **Record**
Make a table with the columns labelled 'object', 'colour in white light' and 'colour through filter'. Fill it in as you view each object.

▶ **Extra experiment**
Attach the red filter to a torch and the green filter to another torch. Shine them both on the white paper. What do you see where the colours overlap?

▶ **What's wrong?**
Can't see a colour change with the torchlight? Make sure both lights shine with the same brightness on the paper.

▶ **Think about it**
Sunglasses use different coloured light filters. What effect do grey lenses have?

Light for sight

Your eye lets you see everything around you, from just in front of your nose to the distant horizon and out into space to the stars! But you wouldn't have sight without light. Light rays pass through your eyeball to a sensitive wall of cells at the back. Here they form an image that is sent to your brain to tell you what you see.

▼ Some animals, such as frogs, have wide eyes to help them see in the dark.

Images from your eyes travel to your brain along a cord called the optic nerve. The place where the optic nerve leaves the eye is not sensitive to light and is called the blind spot.

▲ Sometimes our brains get in a muddle over what our eyes are seeing. That's how optical illusions work. Which of these centre circles looks the biggest?

Getting going

Our eyes are constantly changing as they receive light messages from the world and send them to our brains. Have you noticed how your pupils get bigger in a darkened room? You can test other parts of your eyes with this fish in a bowl trick!

Can you believe your eyes?

1

Draw a simple fish shape on the card. Cut it out. Draw around it on each piece of coloured paper and cut out the coloured fish.

Science box

Small piece of card, 1 sheet each of bright red, green and blue paper, 4 sheets of white paper, pencil, black marker pen, scissors, glue.

2

Draw a black eye on each coloured fish. Take three sheets of white paper and stick one fish to the middle of each.

3

On the fourth sheet of white paper, draw a large fishbowl shape.

4

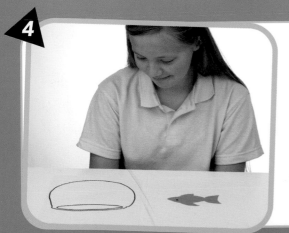

Find a well-lit area. Lie your red fish page next to the bowl page. Stare at the fish eye and count to 20, without blinking, then quickly stare at the bowl.

▶ **Observe**
What do you see when you look at the bowl? What happens to the fish eye?

▶ **Predict**
What will you see with the green fish? What will you see with the blue fish? Test your predictions. Predict and test other shapes and colours. What about a yellow starfish?

▶ **Record**
Make a table to record the colours you see on the white paper each time.

▶ **What's wrong?**
Can't see anything in the bowl? Stare at the fish for longer and don't look anywhere else until it is time to look in the bowl.

▶ **Extra experiments**
Roll a tube out of A4 paper and hold it up to your left eye. Hold your right hand up to the right side of the tube with the palm facing you. What do you see with both eyes open?

▶ **Think about it**
Why do your pupils change size in different lights?

Page 7 Shadowy shapes

The closer the torch is to the object, the bigger and fuzzier the shadow. The shadow is longest when the torch shines at the block from 30 degrees and gets shorter as the angle is increased. There is no shadow at 90 degrees. The shadow of the object changes as the torch is shone on it from different directions. The shape of the shadow will change unless the object is symmetrical like a marble. A clear plastic cup gives a faint shadow because it lets most light through. When two torches are used, each torch produces a shadow.

Page 9 Pinhole pictures

The image on the greaseproof paper screen looks upside down. When you move the camera closer to the subject the image gets larger. Two images are formed by the two holes. More light enters the camera when the hole is enlarged and this makes a brighter but more blurred image. The pictures or images we make in our eyes are upside down. Our brain helps us to see them the right way up.

Page 11 Leaping light

Your bare arm will not reflect light like a shiny watch face. The smooth foil reflects more light than the wrinkled foil. Smooth surfaces reflect more light than rough surfaces. Light colours reflect more light than dark colours, with black reflecting very little light. Black polythene will reflect more light than black paper but less than paler, shiny materials. The light goes from the torch to the test surface then is reflected onto the second white card and then reflected up into your eye.

Page 13 Mirror writing

It's hard to draw and write while looking only in a mirror, because your brain is telling you to do the opposite of what you see. The word CHOICE reads the same in a mirror placed along its length because the letters are symmetrical top to bottom. Other letters that work in this way are B, D, K, X. If you read mirror writing through the back of the paper it looks normal. You can trace over writing from the back to create mirror writing. A small image the right way up is formed in the curved-out surface of the spoon. A larger upside down image is formed in the curved-in surface of the spoon. Rays striking a curved-in surface come together.

Page 15 Peeping periscope

The object should be seen clearly and objects over a wall or other obstacle should also be seen when they are hidden from view when the periscope is not used. When the periscope is lengthened, the image made in the lower mirror will be slightly dimmer if plastic mirrors with scratches are used. You could make a periscope to see behind you by making the top mirror slant in the opposite direction to the bottom mirror and cut a window in the same side as the mirror at the bottom of the box.

Page 17 Cool kaleidoscope

On page 16, 'Getting going', you see multiple images of the pencil (two or three reflections). The pieces in the bag and their reflections in the mirror tube make a pattern. You see this best if you look into a corner part of the tube, which is where the reflections make the pattern appear in a circle. The pattern changes as you twist the tube. The spots of the holographic paper light up in rainbow colours which change as you move the torch around. In 'Think About It', you should see three reflections when the mirrors are placed at 45 degrees. To see more reflections, decrease the angle of the mirrors.

Page 19 Watery wiggle

The angle of the light beam leaving the jar of water is equal to the angle of the beam entering the jar. The beam changes direction when it enters the water at an angle. When it enters at 90 degrees it continues in a straight line. The coin comes into view when water is poured into the bowl because water refracts the 'hidden' image into view. The river will seem shallower than it really is and may be too deep to cross safely.

Page 21 Toy telescope

The view through the telescope comes into focus when the distance between the lenses is equal to the measurement you made in Step 1, and the image you see is upside down. When looking at the book, the first lens magnifies the text and the second lens magnifies it even more – you have made a microscope. A convex lens focuses light inwards.

Page 23 Wheel of wonder

The spinning colours appeared whitish. If you paint only yellow and blue segments, you'll see green. If you paint only red and blue segments, you'll see purple. Our eyes mix the coloured dots of a magazine page or television screen to give the full range of colours we see.

Page 25 Filter fun

Only the red can be seen clearly in the spectrum when viewed with the red filter. Only the blue and the red can be seen clearly in the spectrum when viewed with the blue filter. The picture disappears when viewed through the red filter. All the other colours from the white light from the paper are stopped and the light from the red ink joins the red light from the paper as they pass through the filter. When the red light and the green light from the torches overlap you can see yellow. Grey sunglasses reduce the brightness from light without blocking any colours more than others.

Page 27 Can you believe your eyes?

On page 26, the centre circle on the left looks biggest – but they are actually both the same size. When you look at the bowl after staring at the fish, a faint fish appears in the bowl. This is called an after image. It is made because the light-sensitive cells at the back of your eyes take a few moments to stop recording, so you still see the fish on the blank paper. You'll see an pink after image with the green fish and a yellow/orange after image with the blue fish. In the extra experiment you should see a hole in the centre of the palm of your hand. The pupils change size to control the amount of light entering the eye so you won't be dazzled in bright light and can see a little in dim light.

Further information

Look at these websites for more information on materials and how they change:

▶ http://www.exploratorium.edu/science_explorer/pringles_pinhole.html
Make a pinhole camera from a potato crisp container at this website. You will need an adult to help you, then use the camera and scroll down to the end of the page to find out more about how a pinhole camera works.

▶ http://www.light-science.com/rainlight.html
Read about reflection and then prove that light travels in straight lines by scrolling down to the activity on this website.

▶ http://www.kids-science-experiments.com/shinyspoons.html
Investigate the strange reflections made in spoons at this website.

▶ http://www.guardian.co.uk/science/2008/may/02/physics5
Make a periscope using a different design, with a downloadable template. Now you and a friend can keep an eye on what's going on – perfect for spying over tall fences!

▶ http://www.kaleidoscopecollector.com/mycollection.html
Scroll down to the kaleidoscope artists list at this website and click on any of the names to see beautiful pictures made by kaleidoscopes.

▶ http://www.yorku.ca/eye/rainbow.htm
Find out how rainbows are made at this website.

▶ http://faculty.washington.edu/chudler/chvision.html
A large number of optical activities to try out.

▶ http://pbskids.org/zoom/activities/do/shadowanimals.html
Instructions for making shadows of animals, including a dog, bird and rabbit, just using a torch, your hands and a wall.

Glossary

Absorb light
To take in the energy in light waves.

Binoculars
An instrument composed of two short telescopes – one for each eye.

Cells
Tiny structures that form the bodies of living things. There are many types that perform different tasks. For example, the cells at the back of the eye respond to light waves and send messages to the brain as tiny electrical currents.

Concave
Curving inwards like the inside of a spoon.

Convex
Curving outwards like the surface of a ball.

Filter
A material that absorbs certain colours of light and lets other colours pass through.

Focus
To bring light rays together to a point or to form a clear image.

Image
A picture produced when light rays are reflected from a mirror or focused by a lens.

Laser beam
A beam made from light waves of the same kind that rise and fall together as they move. This makes a very strong concentrated beam of light.

Microscope
An instrument with two or more lenses that magnifies very small objects.

Opaque material
A material that absorbs all the light striking it so that no light can pass through.

Pupil
The circular black hole in the eye through which light passes into the eye.

Reflection
The process in which a light ray bounces off a surface.

Refraction
The process in which a light ray bends as it moves from one transparent substance to another.

Spectrum
The rainbow of colours which can be seen when a beam of light is split up, such as on the surface of a CD.

Telescope
An instrument with lenses, or lenses and mirrors, which make distant objects appear closer.

Transparent material
A material that lets most of the light rays striking it pass straight through.

Translucent material
A material that lets some light pass through but scatters its paths before it leaves.

Index

brains 26
Brewster, Sir David 16

cameras 8–9
colour 4, 22–23, 24–25
concave 13, 20
convex 12, 13, 20

electricity 4, 8
eyes 4, 9, 10, 11, 17, 18,
    21, 24, 26–27

filters 24–25
frogs 26

glasses 20

kaleidoscopes 16–17

lasers 6
lenses 20–21, 25
light cells 4
light energy 4, 8
light rays 6, 8, 10–11,
    12–13, 14, 18–19, 20,
    22, 26
light sources 6, 10–11
light waves 4, 22
long-sight 21

magnifying glasses 21, 23
microscopes 20, 21, 23
mirrors 12–13, 14–15,
    16–17

Newton, Isaac 22

opaque objects 6
optical illusions 26–27
opticians 20
optic nerve 26

periscopes 14–15
photons 4
pupils 26, 27

rainbow 4, 22
reflection 10–11, 12–13,
    14, 22
refraction 18–19, 20, 22

shadows 6–7
spectrum 22, 25
submarines 14
Sun 4, 6, 10, 22

telescopes 20, 21
translucent materials 6
transparent materials 6,
    18–19

water 18–19, 22

To my granddaughter
Pippa May

This edition 2012

First published in 2008 by
Franklin Watts
338 Euston Road
London NW1 3BH

Franklin Watts Australia
Level 17/207 Kent Street
Sydney NSW 2000

Text © Peter Riley 2008
Design and Concept © Franklin Watts 2008

All rights reserved.

Editor: Susie Brooks
Series editor: Adrian Cole
Art Director: Jonathan Hair
Design: Matthew Lilly
Picture Research: Diana Morris
Photography: Andy Crawford (unless
otherwise credited)

Acknowledgements:
David Barrett/Alamy: 18t. Ron Boardman/Frank
Lane Picture Agency/Corbis: 3cl, 20t. Eugene
Buchko/Shutterstock: cover tl. Sascha
Burkard/Shutterstock: 1, 3bl, 26. Jim Cole/Alamy:
12t. Phillip Date/Shutterstock: 2tr, 8.
DWPhotos/Shutterstock: 10-11. Pablo
Eder/Shutterstock: cover cl. Eric
Etman/Shutterstock: cover cr. Christopher
Ewing/Shutterstock: cover br. Owen
Franken/Corbis: 14t. Leslie Garland Picture
Library/Alamy: 3tr, 18b. Eddie Gerald /Alamy:
12b. Laurence Gough/Shutterstock: 2tl, 5t. Anton
Gvozdikov/Shutterstock: 22t. Chris
Hill/Shutterstock: 3cr, 22b. jgl247/Shutterstock:
6l. Michael A. Keller/zefa/Corbis: 20b. Antonio
Lacovelli/Shutterstock: 3clb, 24. Oshchepkov
Dmitry/Shutterstock: cover tr. Alfred Pasieka/SPL:
3tl, 16t. Stijn Peeters/Shutterstock: cover bl.
Photosmart/Shutterstock: 2tc, 6r. Photri /Topfoto:
2br, 14b. E.G.Pors/Shutterstock: cover tc.
QiLux/Shutterstock: 4br. Suzanne
Tucker/Shutterstock: 4 b/g. Craig Tuttle/Corbis:
16b. Serg Zastavkin/Shutterstock: 4bl.
Every attempt has been made to clear
copyright. Should there be any inadvertent
omission please apply
to the publisher for rectification.

A CIP catalogue record for this
book is available from the
British Library.

Dewey number: 535

ISBN: 978 1 4451 0732 5

Printed in China

Franklin Watts is a division of
Hachette Children's Books,
an Hachette UK company.
www.hachette.co.uk